THE ODYSSEY

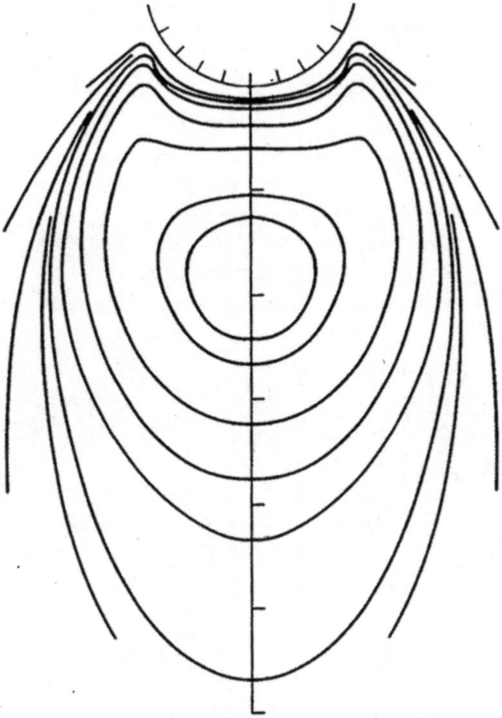

THE ODYSSEY

KEN HUNT

BOOK*HUG PRESS

FIRST EDITION

The production of this book was made possible through the generous assistance of the Canada Council for the Arts and the Ontario Arts Council. Book*hug Press also acknowledges the support of the Government of Canada through the Canada Book Fund and the Government of Ontario through the Ontario Book Publishing Tax Credit and the Ontario Book Fund.

Canada Council for the Arts Conseil des Arts du Canada

ONTARIO ARTS COUNCIL
CONSEIL DES ARTS DE L'ONTARIO
an Ontario government agency
un organisme du gouvernement de l'Ontario

Funded by the Government of Canada Financé par le gouvernement du Canada Canada

Book*hug Press acknowledges the land on which it operates. For thousands of years it has been the traditional land of the Huron-Wendat, the Seneca, and most recently, the Mississaugas of the Credit River. Today, this meeting place is still the home to many Indigenous people from across Turtle Island, and we are grateful to have the opportunity to work on this land.

Printed in Canada

for
Luna's
lost
ones

"I'd like to go back up and erase them."

—Neil Armstrong

(when asked about
the footprints he left
on the Moon's surface)

CONFIDENTIAL

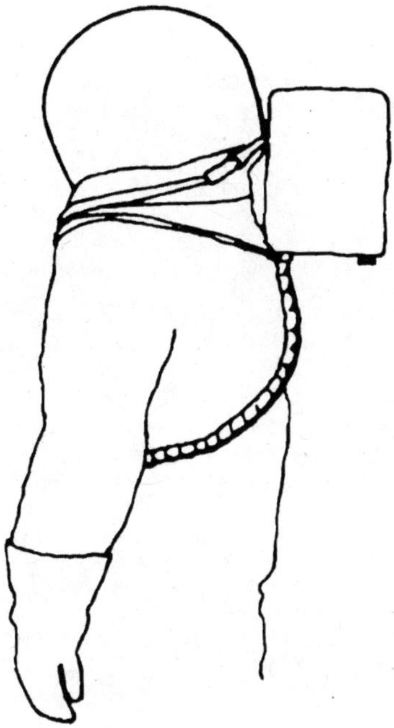

CONFIDENTIAL

I

CONFIDE

ON E

F E T AL

IDE A

I N

A

N E T

O F

CO DE

A

FI N AL

O DE

I N

A

CO I L

O F

D N A

DAY 1:

APOLLO SPACECRAFT

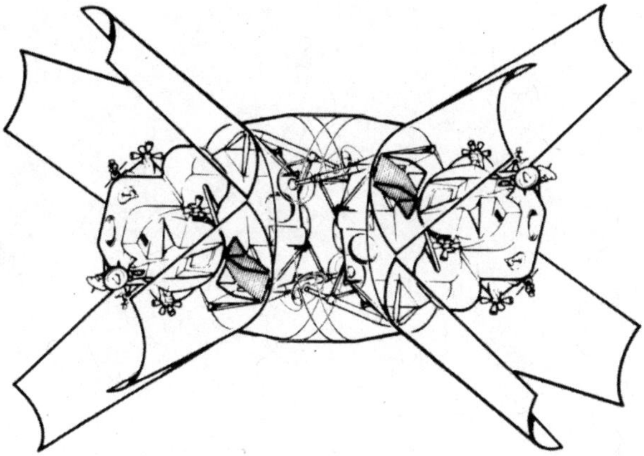

Apollo

transmitted
a

Golden

text

We

Sing

out

IN

the

dark

listen

to

The temperature

drop

a second

of
air

in

an orange dot

slide

your mind over to mine

see

the

white

leak

I got

all

the
way down to

hell
floating

to

you

are you reading

Apollo

We read you

in

angles

That

align

these   optics

point

like   a

whip

in the dark

I see

a

chill in the

ink

We

write

in

looking through

time

the sextant

rules

the stars

lightning

the

body of

noise

We expect

ink

to turn

back

daylight

hold out a

hand

let's

turn

this

into

Gold

in

infinity

it's
not enough

to write what we

know

Minimum

light

inside

your
camera

There are two pieces

There are two pieces

upside down

by looking

to move

the right way

over the

window

of

cloth

a good idea

can get rid of

a good idea

with

a
light

snap

This camera

can

color
a second

on this flight

to

control

light

control

met

doubt

inside

a pen

7 minutes

late for sunrise

you don't see the

body

floating in the aft

a
cell

would be

wise

to
receive

the
king
of
fire

Apollo

a
fire

before

the sun

what the hell   is

                                 he

numbers

change the weight
of time

It's almost the same

It's the same anyway

perfect

ignorance

we're

at

The

apogee

We

don't have any

other

point

to

align

at

on

fire

You

emerge

Burn

the damn flight plan

We

CONTROL

The

VEHICLE

at

the event

time is

circular

on the other side

the numbers

change

you

cells

in the

telescope

adapt

to

sequence

this

world

Apollo

an

Old son

runs cold

A

LUNAR

art

to compute

light

around

Apollo

abort

the

page

to

break your

hand

against

a slow clock

we picked up

your line of sight

thrashing around

the gap

In the

horizon

to write on the wall

I'll cut

And I'll

burn

to

break

this thing we should be reading

Apollo   is

                    light

you feel

this light

          at

          ignition

          in

          flashes

this
dance

in

ashes
lashing out
in

sparks

Apollo

looking

out
at

a
tiny
dot

3 feet per second

everything

Shaking

your face

locked in

this visor

Apollo

I see a bright star out there must be Venus

Venus or

Nothing

at

10 feet per second

the old sun

a hell

I can't   see

14 feet per second   now

we'll be

Just a second

Apollo

We're

a little bit low on time

I got out   I got out

try to get

to   the radio if you can

the event

ate us

the light

rusting

to

ash

going

gray

we

Try to turn off

time

I see a   panel going out

I see

some circuit break

I see

this camera

turned   on

You

Can you see

we're pretty far away from him

How long do we want to run

we turn
toward him

drifting

like spacecraft

ice

closing in

How far are you

     from us   one
                  antenna

          quivers

     we're   close

     we're closing

We

align

And   translate

     probe to spacecraft

PROBE RETRACT

PROBE RETRACT

PROBE RETRACT

PROBE

DEAD

could

a number

Speak

in the

tunnel

where

lips
nap

the

high gain

beam

a

maze
in

sound we

wander

down to

signal

Apollo

DAY 11:

TRANSMISSION RECEIVED

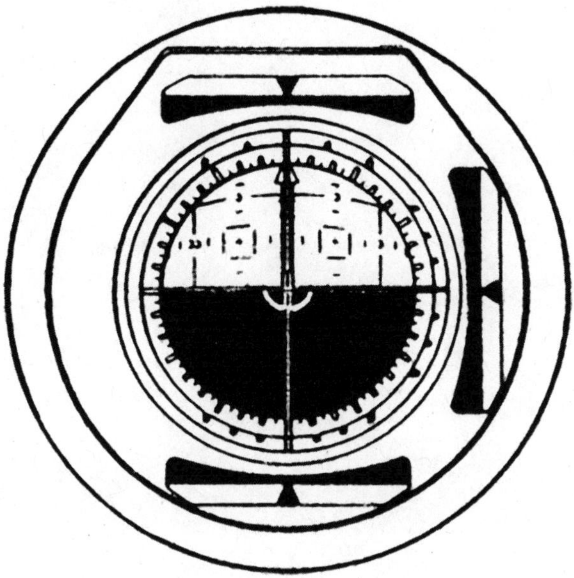

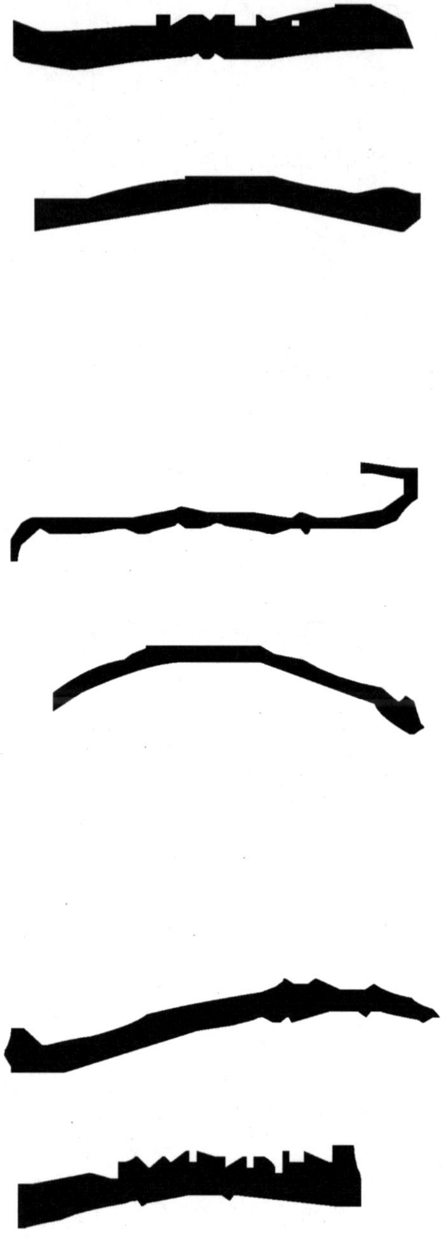

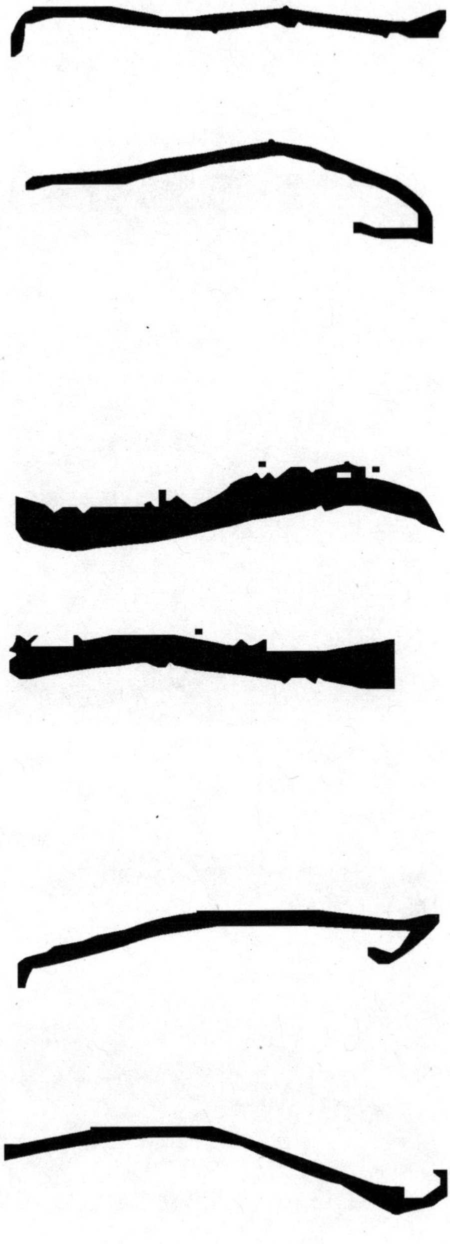

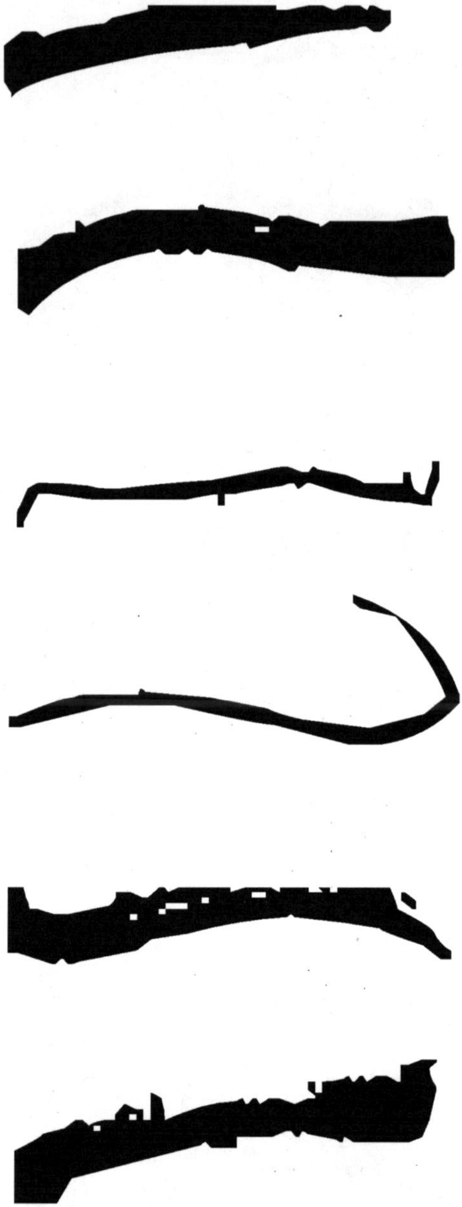

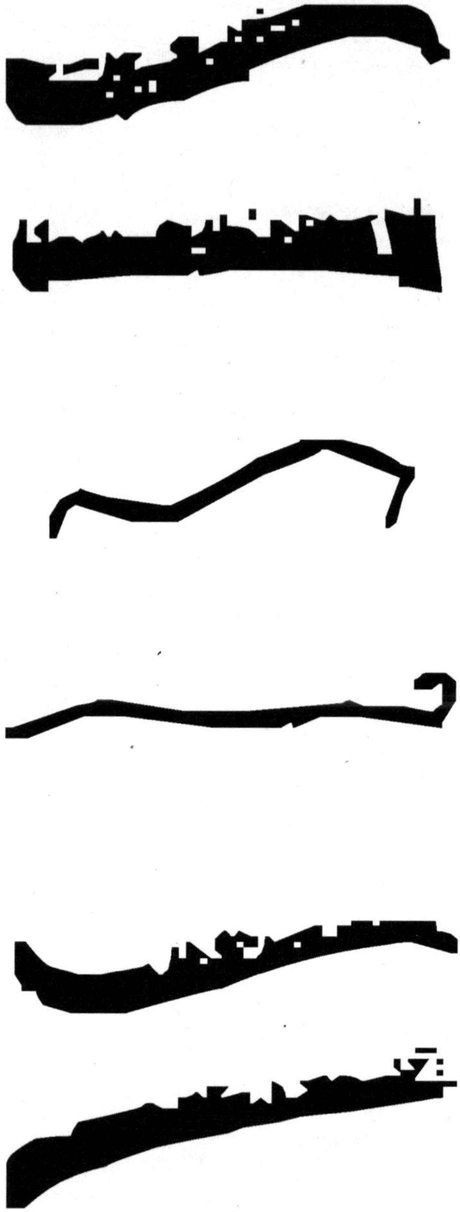

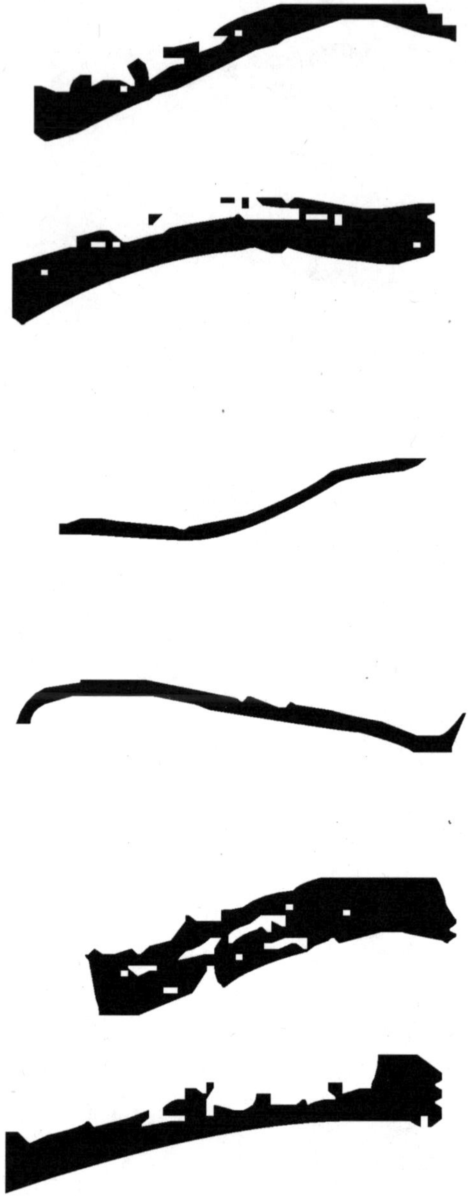

DAY III:

TOP SECRET CALLIGRAPHY

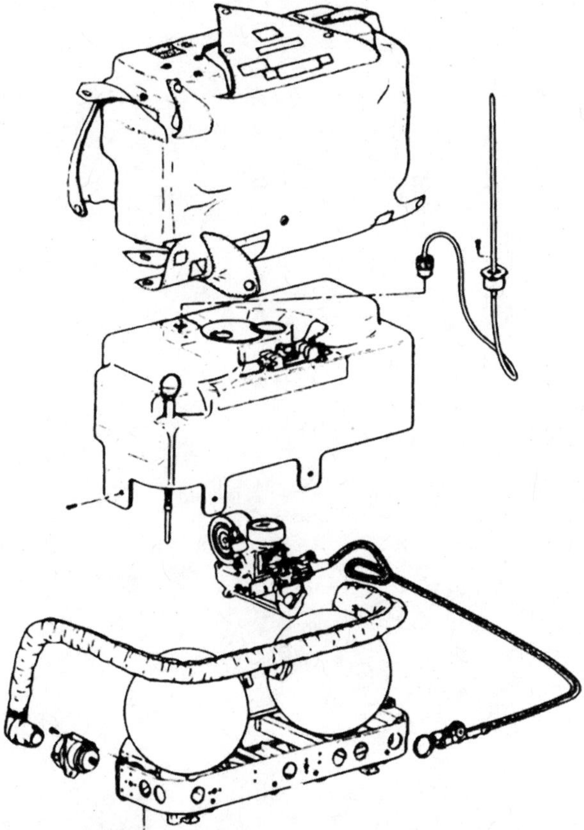

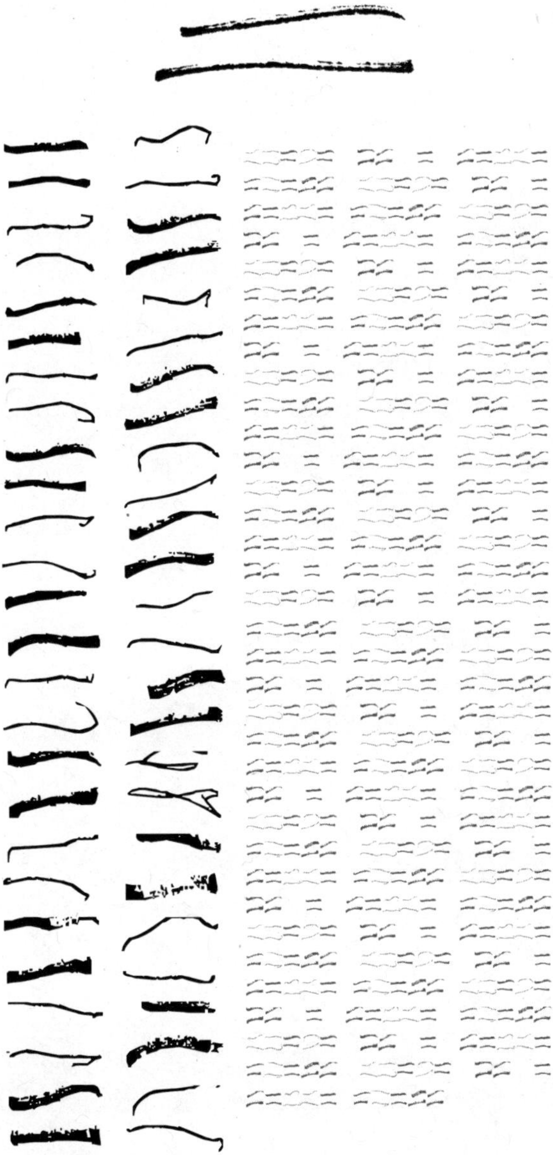

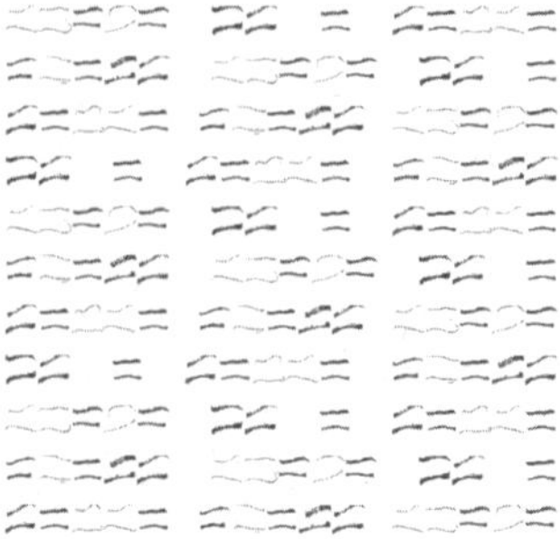

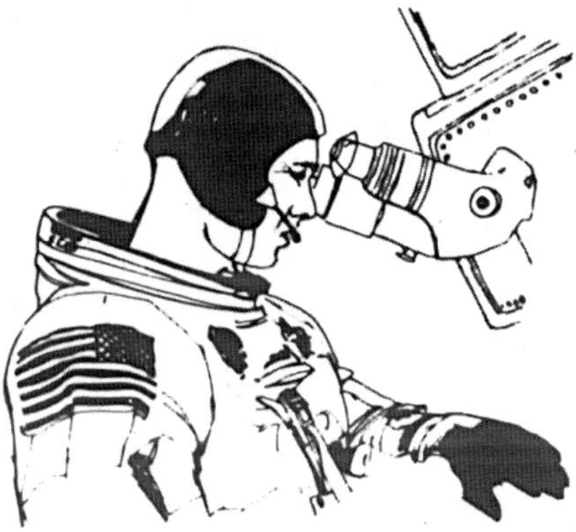

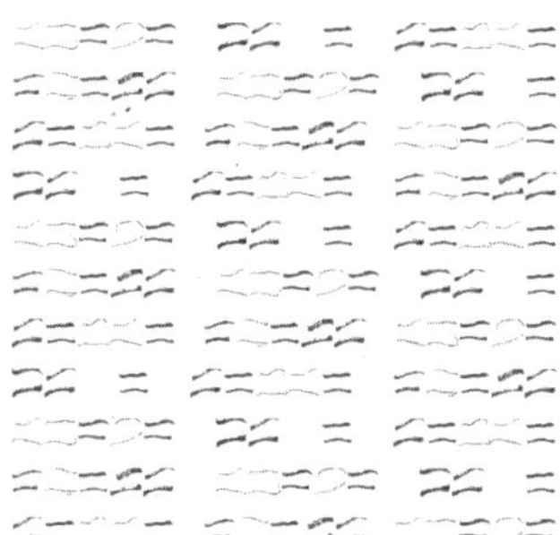

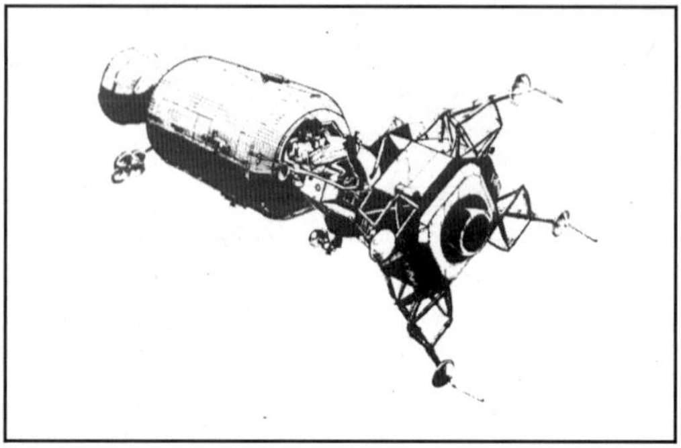

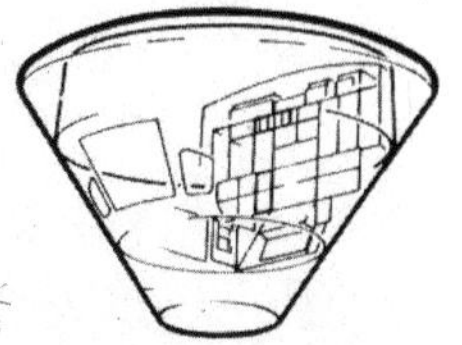

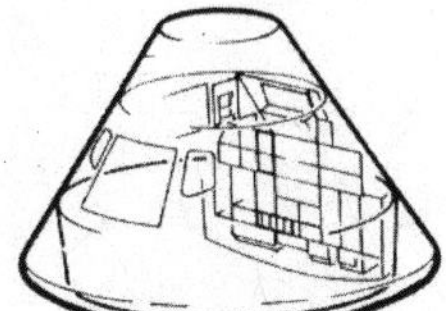

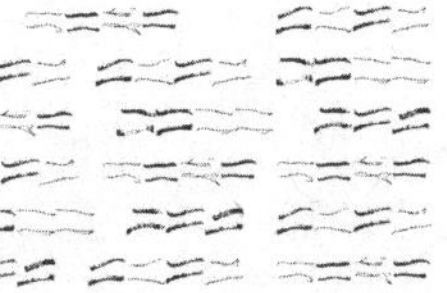

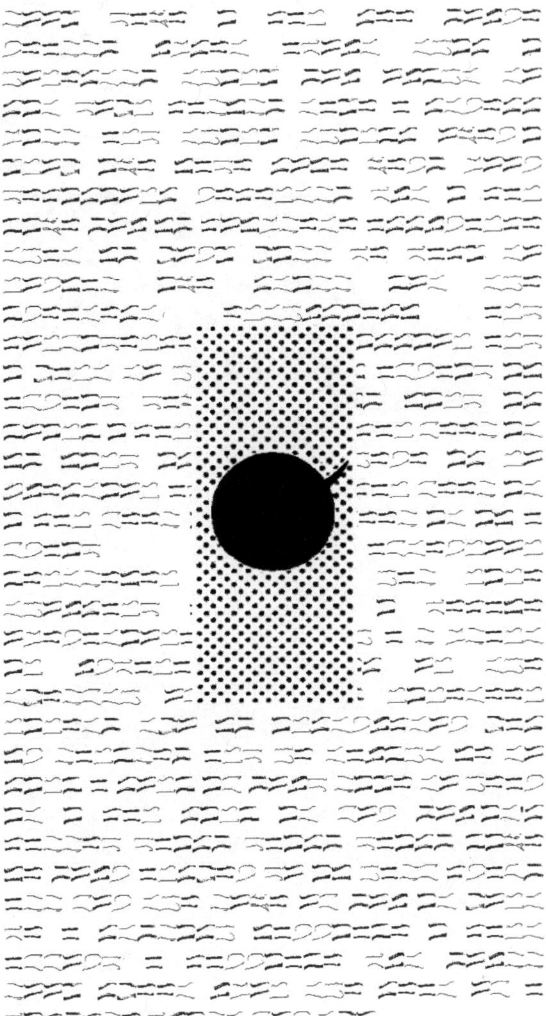

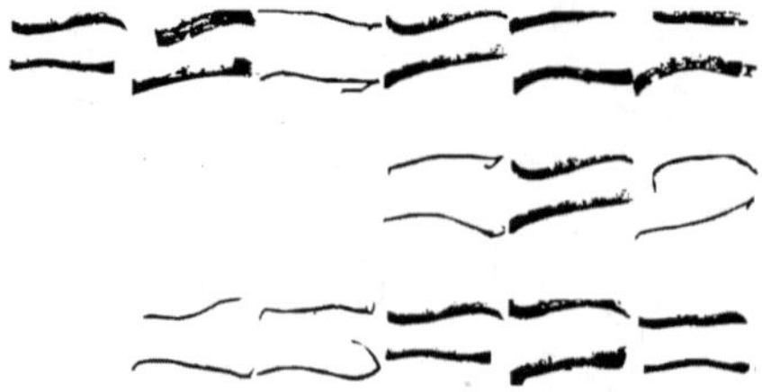

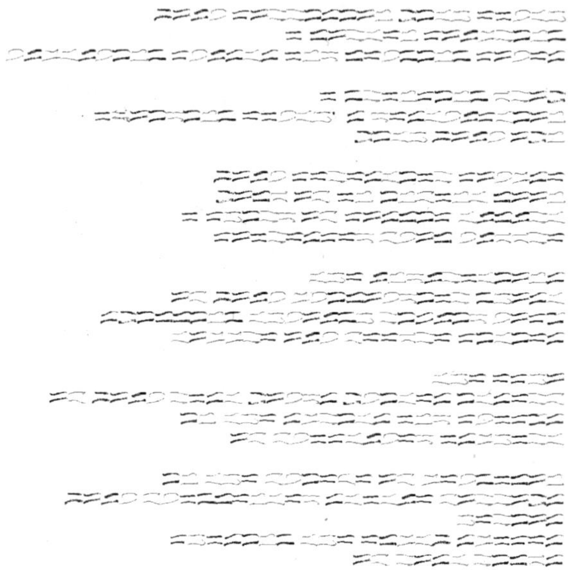

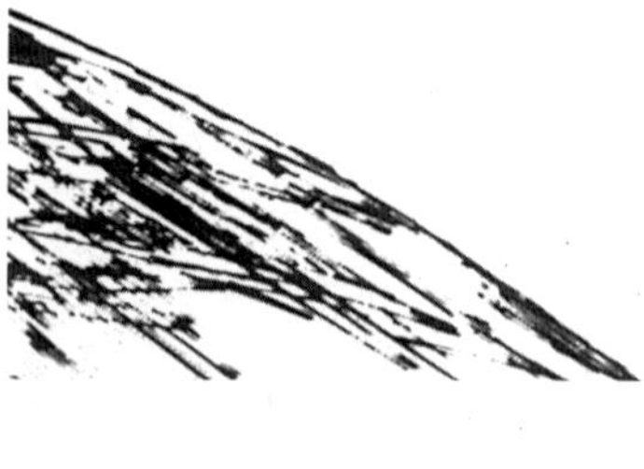

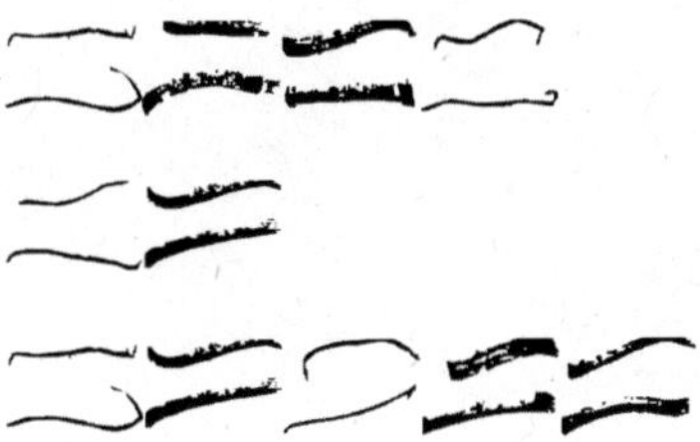

DAY IV:

STATIO TRANQUILITATUS

├ ┌ ┬ ┐ ┤
├ ├ ┼ ┤ ┤
├ └ ┴ ┘ ┤
└ ┴ ┴ ┴ ┘
├ ┌ ┬ ┐ ┤
├ ├ ┼ ┤ ┤
├ └ ┴ ┘ ┤
└ ┴ ┴ ┴ ┘

├ ┌ ┬ ┐ ┤
├ ├ ┼ ┤ ┤
├ └ ┴ ┘ ┤
├ ┌ ┬ ┐ ┤
├ ├ ┼ ┤ ┤
├ └ ┴ ┘ ┤

Apollo

let them

go

the sun

may
corner
you

Look the other way

and

go   to

her

we

come from

the

ink

don't forget us

5 minutes to

Start

her

5 minutes to

lock

you

in

return to

SPACECRAFT

ENTER

SPACECRAFT

the

horizon

blank

the moon

a

Plaster of paris gray

here we come

to

Burn

the

amber

king

below zero

we

feel

a shadow

hold

us

there's a pinging in

the cockpit

where

We

Wander

We

sneak up to

the

dead

is

man

residual

leave

the

light

in her

ink we

spin

as

God

Looks to

her sun

It's a long way

to

the

first

mother

We need a vector

we look

look again

roll 180 and pitch

around her

looking out the   **window**   at the

moon ahead of us

precise

as we

Burn

the earth

we can

take

you

It doesn't matter

if you run

out

to the

black

Moon

your

rough country

ought to be a

book

Give me a

pen

to wash this

map

when you look

at

God

her

dark

lens

pictures

you

look through

her
fused

plane

behind
the mountains
monsters

lie

in

this

fog

we

could spend a lifetime

mother over

mothers

We see the earth

to

view

hell

picture a

clock

on

the moon

you

see

her and

doubt

the flight

should
come

to

earth

We   have

You

          ever   beautiful in the sextant

Apollo   Apollo   you

                      burn us

Apollo   Apollo

why

          this

                      name

We

map

this

last

guess

without

rest

unlock

the rest of this page

And we'll take

pictures of the moon

we

map

the moon

you

wonder where we are

going

Whistling

at

gray

ground

Oh

god

we're going

back to you

You got yourself
an

angle

And we're

reading the

pitch

in

the white

Nothing

look

through

the

star

that

made

you

Leave the

spacecraft

do you have

the power

to leave

did you get

the right numbers

should

we take off

Light the motor

When

seconds

fluoresce

damn

this monstrosity

You can see the horizon

through the

light

boiled off

on the way to the moon

on

black and white film

We

call out to

her

in

a crater the

damned

read us

number to

number

those
cells
carry the

minutes

read for

Her

wise

Clock

what numbers do we

see

if

time

returns to zero

three of them

go
down

shaking

not sure

of anything

all we

got

is

a

pen

he's holding

down

zero is

in control

the tape

is

as close as you're going to get

That

body

behind

you

wait for it to

burn

God damn

what we

say

art

Takes

you

through

hell

observe the lunar surface

Her
bright

white
rim

a

spectacular

picture

nothing more desolate than
these craters

People that live in her

ink

gather
on the edge

of the white

window and look in

at us

I have heard

her

at

the bottom of this
crater
deceiving me

in

orbit

you

face

what

I want to
believe

I don't want to see any more

Who's

over there on the

wall of that crater

slumped down

to watch our

earth

in an infinity

of

ink

you hear

a bright

lie

down in that crater

a

body

eaten away

Apollo

go
to
her

Apollo

looks real   to us

on

film

You

shoot

the wrong one

the right one

The one you want

a piece of

her

rules

my hands

I don't

want to

see her

dark

side

we

miss

her

we

read the

mirror

for

a page

don't

think

about

What

you know

I'm

going to

hell

with the camera

loaded

in the pen

you see a need to

ink

her dust

I'm

able

to

record your

data

But I can't see

you

to

control

space

take

the mission

waiting for

You

earth

on

the horizon

cold in her

hand

They

Check

How

Numb

I feel

going blind

in

the simulator

yawing

toward

hell

for

Apollo

I'll proceed

out of

curiosity

the

flight plan
says
stop

we've gone quite a ways

a

. lunar face

Might

look at

us

for

A beautiful view

damn

You

Apollo

that procedure

was

a flurry of thruster firing

written

out of the

results

you

gave

us

at
the landing site

we

study

triangular roads

at

The crater over there

Can you

see

Apollo the Eagle

looking

eerie

shot down
on the

side of a mountain

We

sleep

for

the

hours

ahead

Apollo   do you read

our   sleep

past

the page

on a
descent

out of the

dark

I can't hear you

Apollo

Apollo
I'm not getting
sleep

Apollo

are you

there?

Apollo   Apollo

Did you hear him answer?

they can hear you

in sleep

and they can   hear me

previous crews have been
here

don't   sleep

lights out
in the

cockpit

the probe

sleeping

over her

don't bring this one back

fix

the

damn

tapes

Luna asleep

in the

ink

A body

of
night

at the last meal we eat

a piece of bread

What are you reading

in

this

ink

you

Found

you adapt
to

the moon

this

hell in your way

you

survive

in

this
System

a dusty vehicle
approaching the landing site

a shadow

curved

her

body

did you

believe

you could dislodge the

night

get

us

out

of here

Anybody

bring back

Apollo

We'll see you on the other side

the paper

rough with water

you remember when they told us

this elaborate scheme

We

have

No

grief

They tell me you got to
the other side

of
light

as

you sleep

the

probe

goes

looking for

you

We went
the next day to

a crater

shooting

in his light

crater walls

like

Seashells

symmetrical

in

hell   the horizon

is

Black

one

dark
shelf

to keep

time

Through

this field of

black

Apollo

appears

we

are

with
her

no
king

can

come this far

put in
a   spare

box

if the computer agrees

We've got

an eye

on

You

hell

            won't hurt

for some

DAY V:

WALTZ WITH LUNA

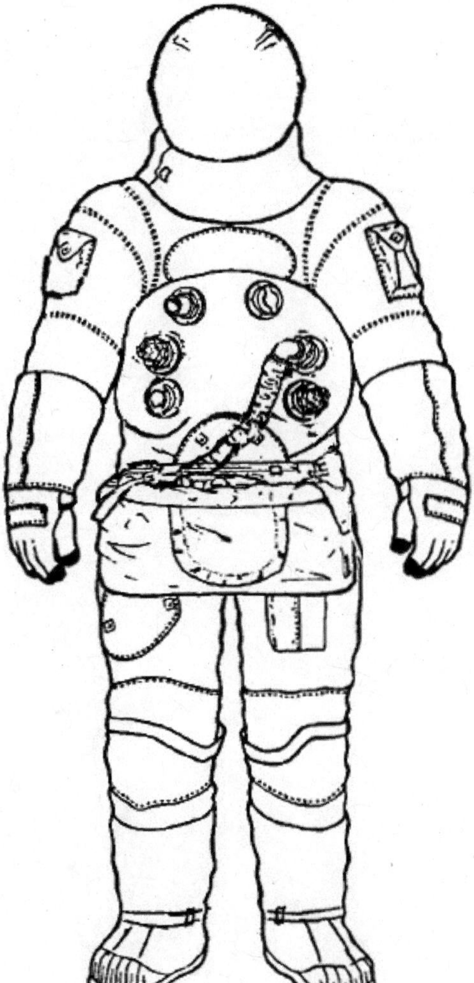

hours

firing

your

camera

to

watch

us

take

wing

out of her

book

do you recall
this recent rust

a body

acting

on

this

Apollo
spacecraft

the probe

you

capture latches

to

you

the timeline you

tunnel

to

is

gone

We

hear

out

in

Her

gray

fire

a pen

click

read

the war

the

Eagle

fed

to reach the earth

we

read

between
coordinates

in a
crater

We sit waiting for
a vector

we watch

you

dance with the page

through the

bright

fire

in
a

Diamond

the landing gear is out

Are those angles

another

lie

How do you read

the dead

copy

this

drifting

program

Beware the revolution

on the lunar surface

you

can see her

dance around
the numbers

the

plan for the

rendezvous

covers

what you say

after you

slip off

That suit

for

100 hours

I've killed
you

in the simulator

I'd prefer you

killed perfectly

you   drift

undocked

tracking light

off

his

fire

ready to

eat

us

let

free

Beautiful

Eagle

Let

us

in

read

the

moon to

us

take us

to

her

The clocks

we keep

Can't change

let
her

write

us

as

We should have been

lose that

tape

underneath this cover

in

hell

we're

lost

because

we

doubt

at the wrong time

maybe a second

off

You

pull

that
circuit breaker

don't

get

lost

the light goes out

You hear

Laughter

like wind whipping around the trees

they were expecting

You

on the page

we

Hear

them

Is your camera running

read

closely

Show us

the

ink

you

leave

in

her

light

look

down

on

the

flag

still

now

in

the window

switch

to

manual

and

Give me

to the

king

We

ward

this

shadow

city

in

dust

drifting

Tranquil her

touch

nearby

optics point at

you

I was unable to see them

pass

behind a
crater

to

scan

us

How do you read

a

mind you broke

I can't see

I can only

weep

DAY VII:

FLIGHT FROM THE DARK

kin

to a king

OF

the

DEAD

stand   by for
             the

dance

that

shadow

in

front of us

Do you see the

ink

wallowing

Within

in

the city

of

Eve

I
glimpse

her

a pen

the ENGINE

for

our

king

You

break

alignment

leaving behind
Apollo and

the

pen

are

We the
First

to hear

you

you man

the

Eagle

and

in

seconds

We're burning

which way did

you

structure

our story

We see the light

cry

holes in

us

Think
up
a solution

damn it

they

remember

the way

we

film

her

ash

sweeps

over

the

ink

Did you Burn

us

for a

reason

I can't see you

I can't see

It doesn't show up in the   books
                                   the

data

On the

Last

tape

and   in

             us

after

you

burn

it's not

over

in the sunlight

I see you

fused to

this data

a last

laugh

at

two bright spots

we are

a

shape of

light

sing

through

us

on other spacecraft

in

the

ice

the

crews

I remember

losing

I don't know why I lost my

wish

for

Flying

are you

going to

lie

I

Hope you know how

to end a

war

left

on

earth

you

view

us

in

the

ink

to

contact you

We make

this

radar

in the

water

things

could

watch

you

Use

lithium

They
mentioned

pills

I know

the

Laughter

of

the moon

in

that

sample

you can see them

like powdered graphite

a crew

we want to take back

we're going to
get you out of here

throw
out the data

they're in

your circuit

the book you

leave
her

We see

as theory

I

had

the

probe

open

to reach

My ears from

inside

you hear a noise

during lift-off

see

a bunch

of

dust

spray out
and engulf

the

ship

what stuck to the spacecraft

is it basalt dust?

We

hear

The

damned

in the rocks

for years

you

don't know

your

way home

in
a
suit you

take this

final

walk

when you walk
out of the

ship

you look almost white

on earth

we

set the clock

for the end

the rocks scurried

around them

this is geology

we

don't kno

you've seen

her

in

the wall of

ink

in

orbit

We're in

wonder

on the other side

I heard him call

for

you

Somehow we'll

maintain

the data that shows

contact

the film

could

stay locked

in here

We

connect
to
god
with

ink

invent a new home

for the tape

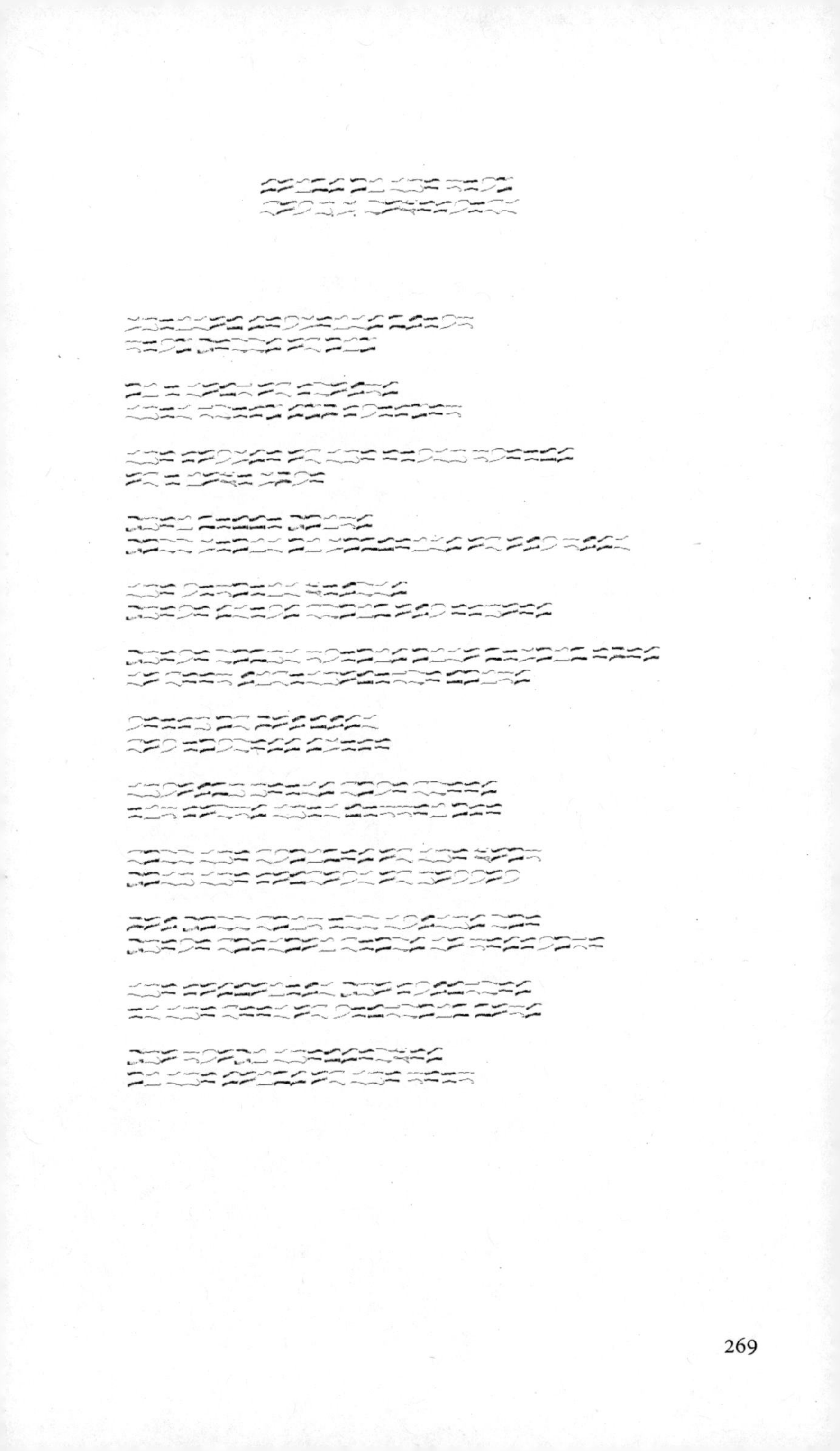

king

of

fire

damned

to

ashes

until the debriefing

I never thought about

one of them

Purring across the deep

with a camera

I'll take

from the moon

all

her

horizon

lines

in

one eye

you
eye

the

king

in
fire

Oh
hell

It
can think

Question the computer

press on

in

an ode

to

spacecraft

Twelve of them

lost

in

wonder   on

the moon
give us

her

boiling

cold

horizon

the

hopeless

Shades of

hades

escape

hell

after

us

You won't be able to see

when

the

moon

looks

for

you

be

numb

When the

minutes

read

Go

Verify

are they

in

us

Verify

Do i look right

out to your

urn

We

three

Proceed

this damn
lie

a perfect
simulator

believe

in

blanks

Burn

the

dead

king

in amber

light

nitrogen

pressure's falling

brace yourself

record the

dance

a residual

jewel

keep the moon in sight

proceed

to

the

spacecraft

You've

been changed

her

laughter

Isn't

a

call

to the

moon

We have a damned program ready to

hatch

This

singing

tape in

black and white

I've seen enough

today

we

burn

the camera

UNNOVAE

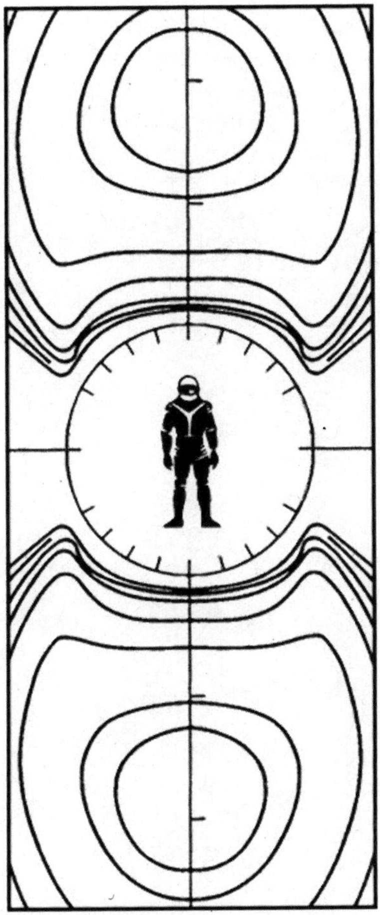

EONS I SEE

For Galileo Galilei

.

--

-- .

.

E .

.

.

.

o ns .

.

I

.

s e e .

.

.

.

-

er .

a .

s -

. e .

.

.

STATIO TRANQUILLITATUS

For Mary Ellen Solt

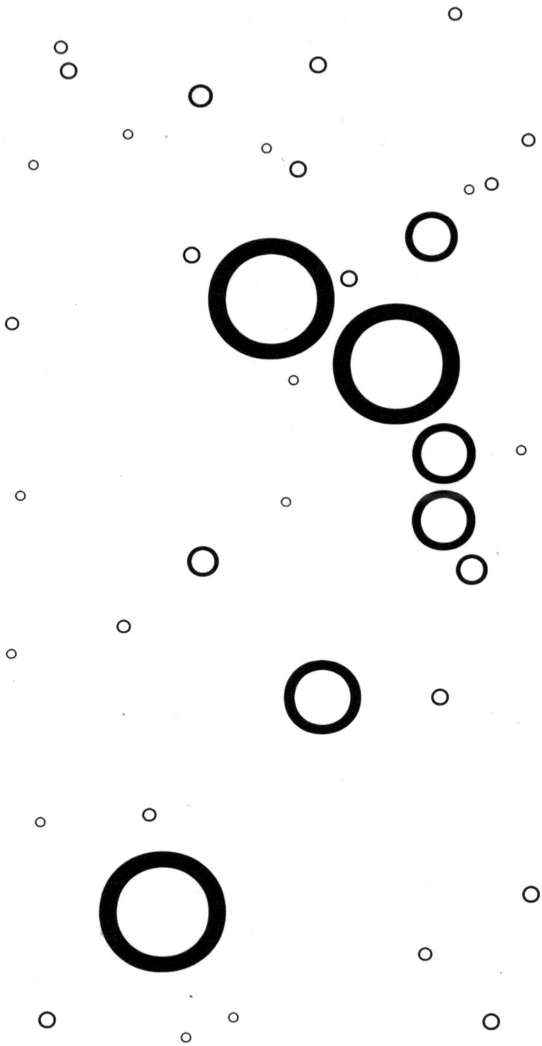

DAISY KNELL

For Arthur C. Clarke & Stanley Kubrick

d b

g

d

e f g

e

g

d

a

d

b

g e f

g a

b

a

WOW! SIGNAL

For Jerry R. Ehman

1 4 2

0

.

w

3 5

o w

6 -

1 4

2

0

.

4

5

5

6

SPACE ADMINISTRATION

SPACECRAFT

The Odyssey plunders NASA's voice transcription document (a chronicle of the first six days of the Apollo 11 mission), erasing words in order to find the poetry embedded in the combined code phrases, offhand remarks, and technical jargon spoken by astronauts Neil Armstrong, Buzz Aldrin, and Michael Collins on their pioneering voyage to the moon.

In terms of process, the uncovered text of *The Odyssey* reimagines erasure as a kind of "spacecraft"—(which is to say, the "crafting of space"). Various process and design decisions in *The Odyssey* apply additional constraints to the typical erasure method, with the aim of improving the resulting poems. Firstly, *The Odyssey* utilizes a 4-column grid, which each word in the erasure poems is "snapped to." This alters the words' horizontal positions, refining the aesthetic of the poems while preserving the words' vertical positions (a.k.a, the order in which they appear within the original NASA document). Secondly, *The Odyssey* avoids cobbling together new words of two letters or more using single letters from existing words. This means that each poem contains only "whole" or "complete" terms, either repurposed in their original state or "dug out" of longer words. Thirdly, each page of the erasure strives, whenever possible, to create a grammatically "complete" sentence or, at the very least, a cogent phrase. To achieve this, two-page spreads occasionally string together a sentence in two parts. Fourthly, an effort was made to utilize deific terms such as "Apollo," "Luna," "God," "light," etc., whenever possible. Finally, the poems in *The Odyssey* strive to refer to their own construction via the process of erasure, as well as to comment upon the act of reading and the reader's role in the creation and interpretation of the text. In order to operate within these constraints, the majority of *The Odyssey*'s pages required between 10 and 25 distinct attempts at erasure in order to achieve the current version of the manuscript.

Visually, the poems of *The Odyssey* perform an inversion of the cosmos, in which pinpoints of light disobey the dark veil of space. The poems become dark constellations of words suspended in a void of light, cryptic maps that guide the eye through celestial labyrinths conceived by the all-too-human impulse to seek patterns in chaos. In print, the typewritten text of the NASA source document, legible but slightly decayed due to the state of the documents at the time of their digitization, showcases the odd distressed or cracked letter. These weary glyphs call to mind the concrete poetry of derek beaulieu, who fashions textual sculptures out of scraps of letraset. Conceptually, the text performs elegiac calls to Apollo, the god of poetry, and Luna, the goddess of the Moon, who dwell in the empty spaces of the page. These poems portray Apollo and Luna as allied alien deities who consume interstellar conquerors whose voyages favour dominance over discovery. The book likens the experience of the reader of erasure to that of an astronaut, exploring a void whose minimal matter must be clung to for survival. The eye, as it migrates from letter to letter, must rely on the vectors established by the positioning of the letters, a navigation of space that the poems themselves acknowledge and comment upon. As the days of the Apollo 11 mission progress, the poems comment upon encounters with unearthly beings, conspiracies surrounding the original footage of the mission, and the sublime and humbling experience of exploring a cosmos that our human bodies struggle to grapple with despite extensive technological assistance.

MISSING TIME

Unlike the other days chronicled in the Apollo 11 voice transcription document, days 2 and 3 of the mission are not available online as PDF scans of older hard copies. There exists at least one website containing a digital record of this portion of the mission. However, this portion of the mission not only lacks the aesthetic of the typewritten portions of the mission transcript, it also lacks the perceived material "authenticity" of a scanned document. Erasing these days as if they were available in the same format as the others would mean ignoring the odd discrepancy between how days 2 and 3 of the Apollo 11 mission were released to the public and the way in which the other days of the mission were made available.

Consequently, days 2 and 3 of *The Odyssey* plunder the visual aspects of NASA's Apollo documents rather than their textual aspects. These sections create a kind of "asemic alphabet" utilizing the strikethroughs used to cross out the word "confidential" on the first 26 pages of the Apollo 11 voice transcription document. This "Top Secret Calligraphy" exemplifies the creation of a new text via the "re-censorship" of the NASA document that the erasure process essentially performs.

Page 224 of the NASA Voice transcription is oddly absent from the scanned PDF of the document, possibly due to having been redacted for undisclosed reasons. In response to this, the page of *The Odyssey* that would have contained an erasure of page 224 instead hosts an asemic poem written in the strikethrough alphabet that was created for the sections representing days 2 and 3.

The images found in the sections of *The Odyssey* that represent days 2 and 3 of the mission are sourced from NASA's online archives of Apollo mission equipment diagrams and technical schematics, including the recently-restored Apollo 11 Press Kit.

STOWAWAYS

The title page of "Day 4" contains Mary Ellen Solt's visual poem "Moon Shot Sonnet," a work derived from the visual grid used by cameras on the Apollo 11 lander. "Eons I see," derived from page 43 of the voice transcription, resulted from a search for phrases that appeared, both in letters and in Morse code, within the source document. "Statio Tranquilitatus" is a visual poem, composed of the letter "o," which mimics the distribution of lunar craters near the Apollo 11 landing site. "Daisy Knell," derived from page 97 of the source document, uncovers the notes of the opening lines of "A Bicycle Built for Two," the death knell of the computer HAL featured in Stanley Kubrick and Arthur C. Clarke's 1968 film *2001: A Space Odyssey*. "Wow! Signal," derived from page 115 of the source document, finds the exact frequency, in both numbers and Morse code, of an incredibly strong radio transmission detected in 1977 at Ohio's Big Ear radio telescope, along with the word "wow."

An earlier draft of "Day 1" of *The Odyssey* was published online and exhibited in print 2014 by the Luma Foundation's *89+ Project*, as a book entitled *Space Administration*. A series of asemic, visual poems derived from the "confidential" strikethroughs was published by derek beaulieu's No Press as a chapbook entitled *Top Secret Calligraphy*. The poem "Daisy Knell" was also published by No Press, as a chapbook of the same name. Poems from *Space Administration* also appear in *Matrix Magazine*.

ACKNOWLEDGMENTS

This book would not exist were it not for the creative contributions and supportive efforts of several individuals. I offer my utmost thanks to my mentor, Christian Bök, for his invaluable criticism over the course of this project's inception and revision. My thanks to Jay and Book*hug for accommodating my idiosyncrasies, to Gregory Betts for going over an early draft of the manuscript, to Robert Majzels for kindling the initial idea, to derek beaulieu for his continued support, to everyone in English 598/698 at the University of Calgary for their constructive suggestions, to my family for their unearthly support, and finally to my partner Nicole for keeping me warm and breathing while we drift through the void.

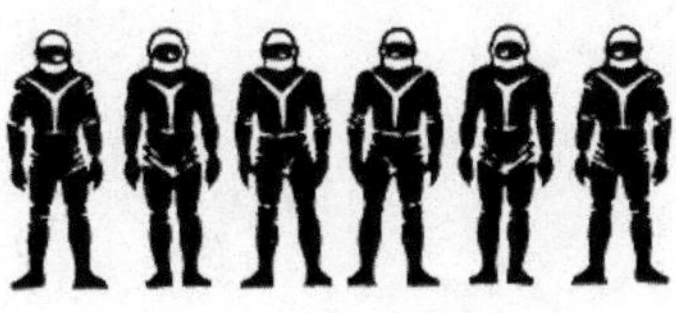

Ken Hunt's writing has appeared in *Chromium Dioxide*, *No Press*, *Matrix*, and *Freefall*. For three years, Ken served as managing editor of *NōD Magazine*, and for one year, as poetry editor of *filling Station*. Ken holds an MA in English from Concordia University and is the founder of Spacecraft Press, an online publisher of experimental writing inspired by science and technology. The LUMA Foundation published his first book of poetry, *Space Administration*, in 2014. His second book of poetry, *The Lost Cosmonauts*, was published by Book*hug Press in the fall of 2018. Ken is a PhD candidate at the University of Western Ontario.

COLOPHON

Manufactured as the first edition of *The Odyssey*
in the summer of 2019 to commemorate
the 50th anniversary of the
Aollo 11 Lunar Mission
July 1969

Book + Cover Design by Ken Hunt